MANNERS *of the* HEART

STUDENT WORKBOOK

Student Activity Sheets & Home Connection Letters

GRADE 1

RESPECT

This book belongs to:

_____

Published by **MANNERS** of the **HEART**

763 North Boulevard
Baton Rouge, LA 70802
225.383.3235
www.mannersoftheheart.org

Third Edition
Copyright 2020 by **MANNERS** of the **HEART**
All rights reserved.
Printed in the United States of America.

Author: Jill Rigby Garner
Editor: Angelle High
Editor at large: Angelle Roddy
Graphic Design: Shelby Bailey, Loren Barilleau
Cover Design: Brian Rivet
Merryville Stories: Nick and Jill Garner, Micah Webber, Janie Spaht Gill, Ph.D.
Contributor: Emily Jones
Photography: Darlene Aguillard, McCauley Mills, Taylor Frey

MANNERS of the **HEART** grants teachers the right to photocopy the reproducibles from this book for classroom use. No other part of this publication may be reproduced, stored in a retrieval system, or transmitted in any form or by any means—electronic, mechanical, photocopy, recording, or any other, without the prior written permission of the publisher. Please direct all questions and inquiries to:

info@mannersoftheheart.org or
MANNERS of the **HEART**
763 North Boulevard
Baton Rouge, LA 70802
www.mannersoftheheart.org

STUDENT ACTIVITY SHEETS

Student Activity Sheet - Week 1

Manners of the Heart

Others can tell what is in your heart by what you say and do.
Fill the heart with good things!

_____
Name

Student Activity Sheet - Week 1

Map of Merryville

Student Activity Sheet - Week 2

Wise Ol' Wilbur

Draw and color a portrait of Wilbur!

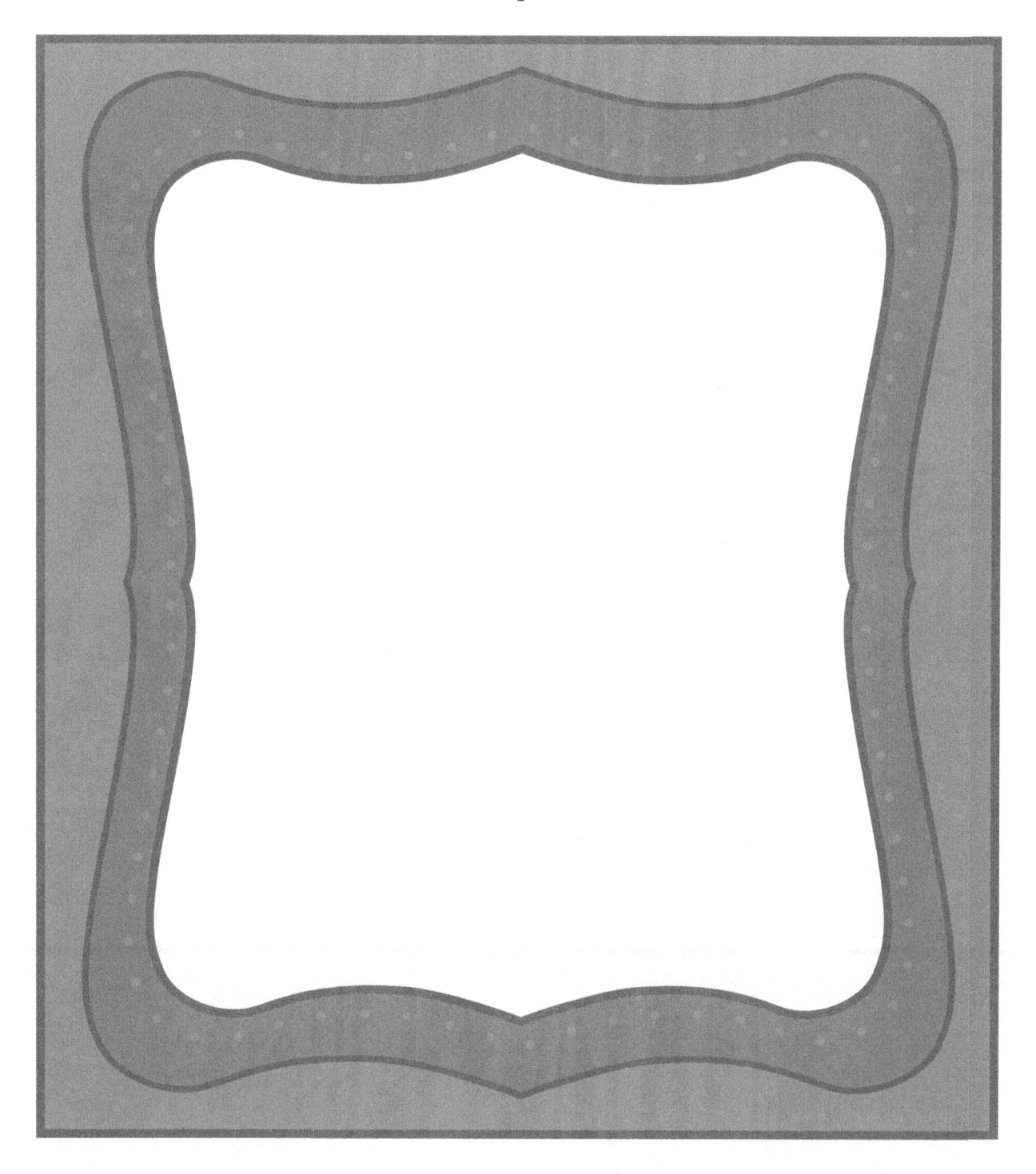

_____
Name

Student Activity Sheet - Week 2

Good Deeds

Let's read the Good Deeds song together!

I'll keep my hands to myself
And my feet on the ground.
I'll raise my hand to talk
Without making a sound.
I'll listen to my teacher,
So I'll know what to do.
I'll do the right thing
For Wilbur and you!

Name

Student Activity Sheet - Week 3

RESPECT

Draw a picture of one person showing respect to another person.

Name

Student Activity Sheet - Week 4

Duty Chart

List each of your duties at home. Check or color the box when you complete a duty on that day.

Duties:	Sunday	Monday	Tuesday	Wednesday	Thursday	Friday	Saturday

Name

Student Activity Sheet - Week 4

The Eyes of Your Heart

Draw a pair of eyes inside the heart!

_____
Name

Student Activity Sheet - Week 5

From a Frown to a Smile

Cut out and glue the face to a paper plate or practice drawing it on your own!

Name

Student Activity Sheet - Week 5

Saying I'm Sorry

Color the heart and write your name!

_____
Name

Student Activity Sheet - Week 6

Gold Words

Cut out the Gold Words and place them into your treasure sack!

- You're Awesome!
- Way to Go!
- Good job!
- Cheer for you!

Name

Student Activity Sheet - Week 8

The Golden Ruler

Color and cut out the Golden Rulers. Tie yarn in the holes to make a hanger. When you are done, you will have one for you and one to give to a friend!

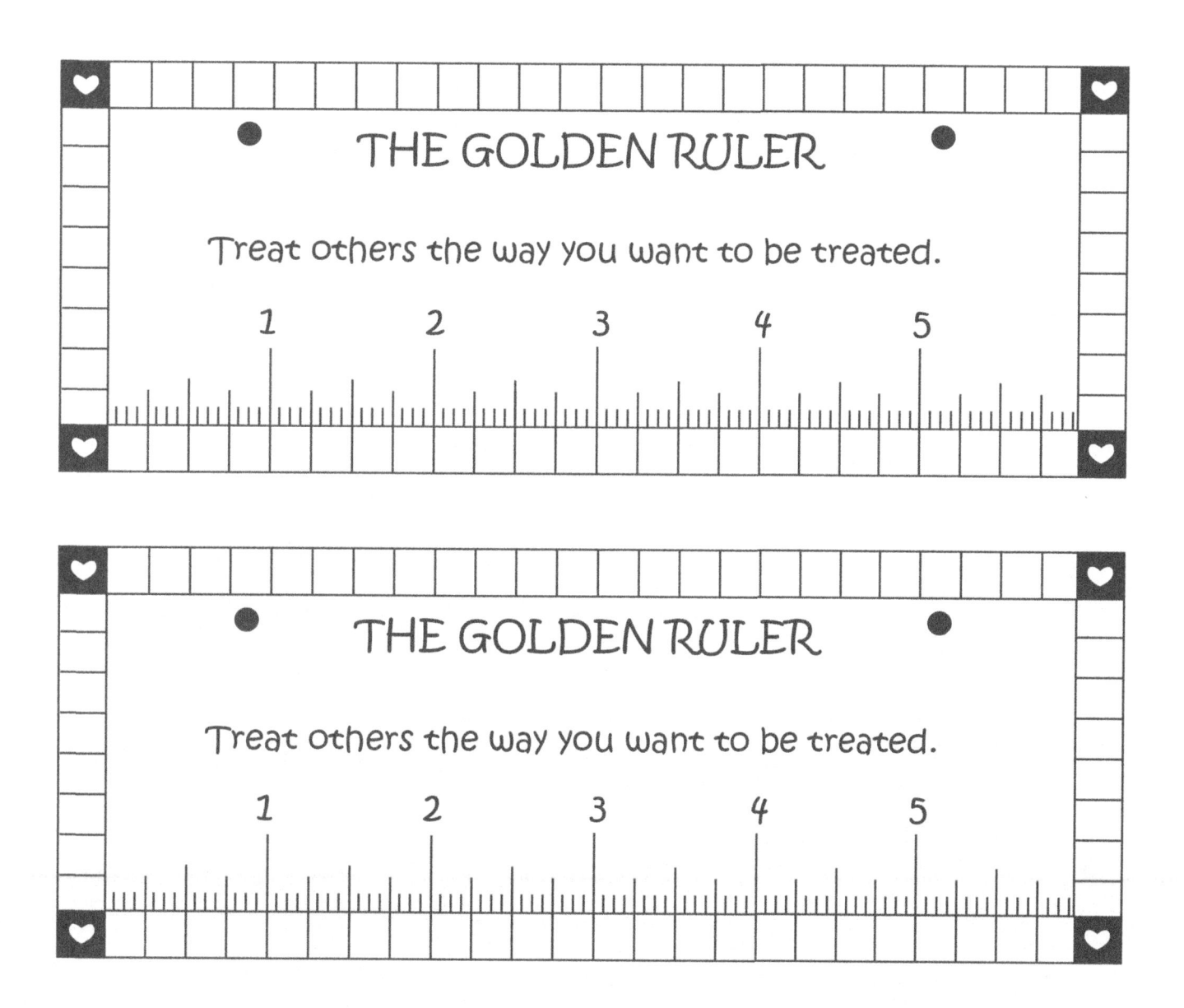

THE GOLDEN RULER

Treat others the way you want to be treated.

1   2   3   4   5

THE GOLDEN RULER

Treat others the way you want to be treated.

1   2   3   4   5

Name

Student Activity Sheet - Week 8

Chocolate Chip Cookie

Cut out the two cookies and put them on your plate!

_____
Name

Student Activity Sheet - Week 9

Paper Crown

Color the crown and cut it out. Then, put the crown together!

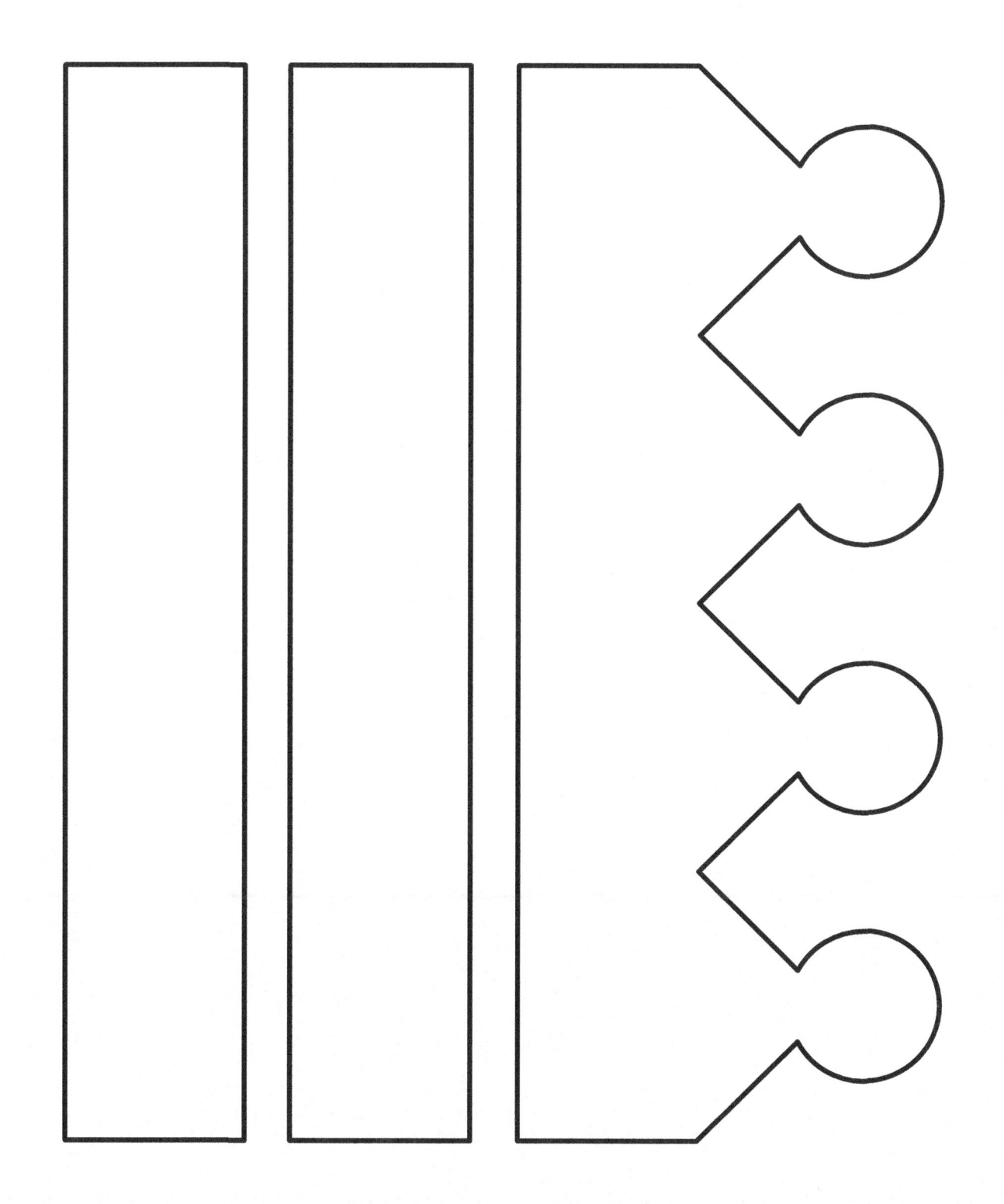

Name

Student Activity Sheet - Week 10

Birthday Cake

Write your birthdate and how old you will be turning, then draw that number of candles on your cake.

_____
Name

Student Activity Sheet - Week 12

SEE, SMILE, STEP, SHAKE, SPEAK

What should you do when you meet someone?

You'll meet a friend once-in-a-while; be sure to greet them with a smile!

S __ __

S __ I __ E

S __ __ __

S H __ K __

S __ E A __

_____
Name

Student Activity Sheet - Week 14

Chatterbox

Color and cut out the phone. Glue your phone onto an index card.

12:45

_____'s Phone

Student Activity Sheet - Week 15

Thank You Card

Cut out the card and fold it in half. Draw a picture on the front.
On the inside, write Thank You! Love, (your name).

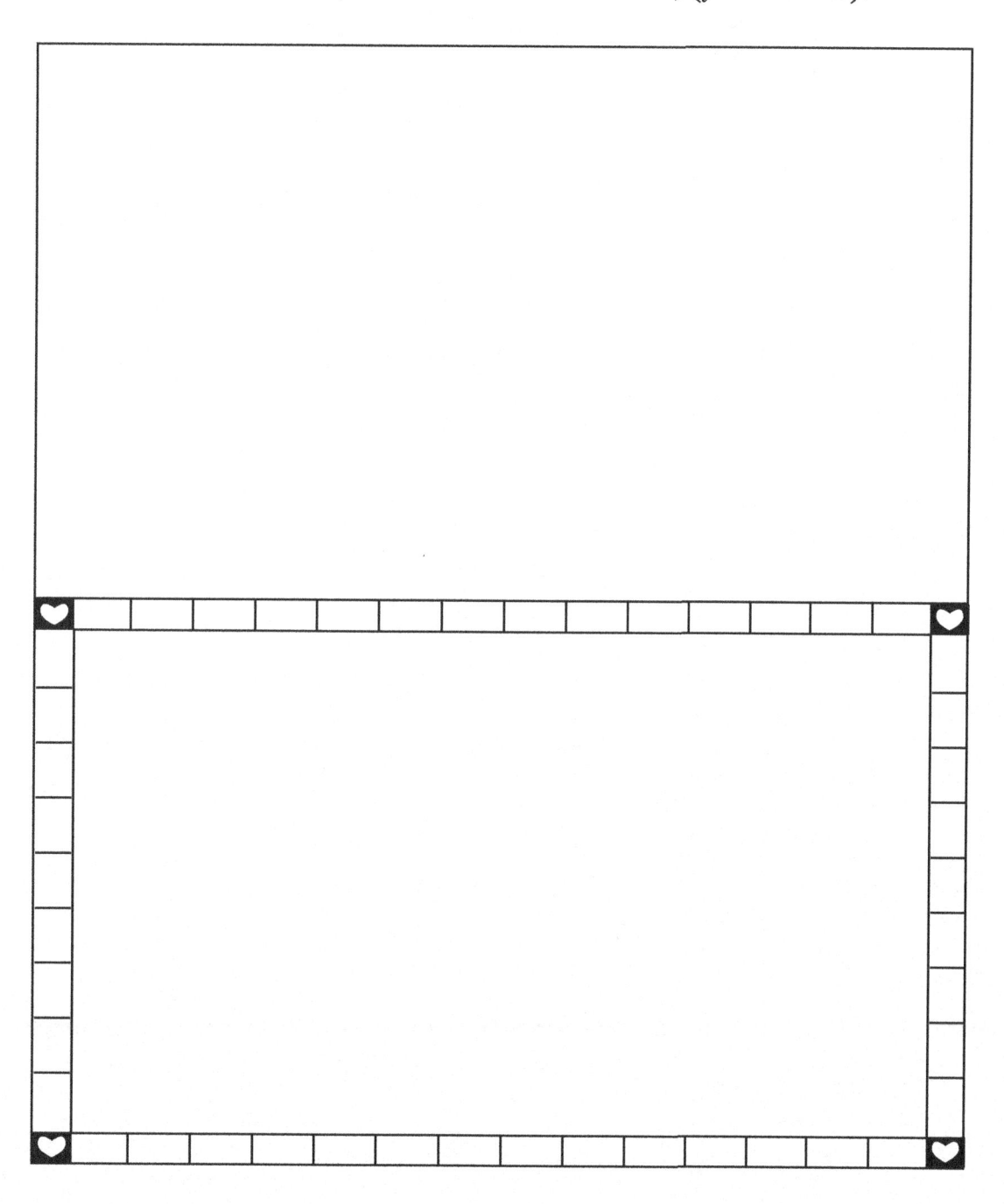

Name

Student Activity Sheet - Week 16

Our School's VIP

Draw a portrait of an adult VIP (Very Important Person) and write their name in the box at the bottom.

Name

Student Activity Sheet - Week 16

Respect for Adults

Put the first letter of the sentence in each block and learn how to respect ADULTS!

- ☐ Answer questions
- ☐ Do what they say
- ☐ Use their correct title
- ☐ Look and Listen
- ☐ Turn your frown upside down
- ☐ Say "Sir" and "Ma'am"

___ ___ ___ ___ ___ ___ ___ ___

Name

Student Activity Sheet - Week 17

Team Player

Draw a line from the name of the sport to the equipment used for it. Circle and color your favorite. Write the name of your favorite sport on the line below.

Basketball

Hockey

Football

Volleyball

Tennis

Ping Pong

Golf

Pool

Baseball

Bowling

Soccer

My favorite sport is: _____

_____
Name

Student Activity Sheet - Week 19

My Favorite Thing

Draw a picture of one of your favorite belongings.
How would you feel if someone borrowed it without your permission?

Name

Student Activity Sheet - Week 20

What a MESS!

Draw a picture of your room as a complete mess!

_____
Name

Student Activity Sheet - Week 21

Just Act Respectfully

Cut out the squares and place them into a jar!

If there is a long line to buy tickets, how should you wait in the line? Wait patiently and quietly. Do not skip anyone; do not push anyone or fool around in the line.	**When there is a crowd of people in a movie theater that you need to get through, you do not shove, but rather say…** Please excuse me!	**If you really need to get up during the movie, how should you exit the theater?** Say "Excuse me" to the people next to you. Do not block the view of people behind you. Exit quickly and quietly.	**What are some gross noises that you should NOT make when at the movies?** [Let them be silly for just a moment with this and then remind them not to make these noises when out in public!]
Show me the kind of voice you should use when at the movie theater… Your inside voice! (No yelling!)	**If a movie theater employee asks you a question, how should you answer?** Speak clearly and say "Sir" and "Ma'am."	**After the movie, what should you do with your food or drink?** Throw it away! Don't leave it for someone else to clean!	**Should you use your cellphone or tablet while the movie is playing?** No! If there is an emergency, walk out of the theater before you use it.
What are some things you can do to quietly eat your food while the movie is playing? No slurping. Quietly unwrap your candy. Chew popcorn with your mouth closed.	**Should you use the restroom before the movie starts, or wait until you really need to go?** Always use it before (even if you don't "need to" yet). Otherwise, you will get up during the movie.	**Show me how you should sit when you are in the movie theater…** Keep arms and legs in your own space! Do not put your feet up on the seats, and do not kick the seat in front of you.	**What are some things to remember when exiting the theater?** Do not block the aisle. Wait for your turn to exit. Don't push.
Should you talk while the movie is playing? No! Only whisper when it is an emergency.	**If you accidentally spill your drink or food, you should…** Clean it up!	**Should you walk or run in the movie theater?** Always walk! You might hurt someone.	**What do you say to the person who paid for your ticket?** Thank you! I had fun!

_____
Name

Student Activity Sheet - Week 22

Thank You Card

Cut out the card and fold it in half. Draw a picture on the front.
On the inside, write Thank You! Love, (your name).

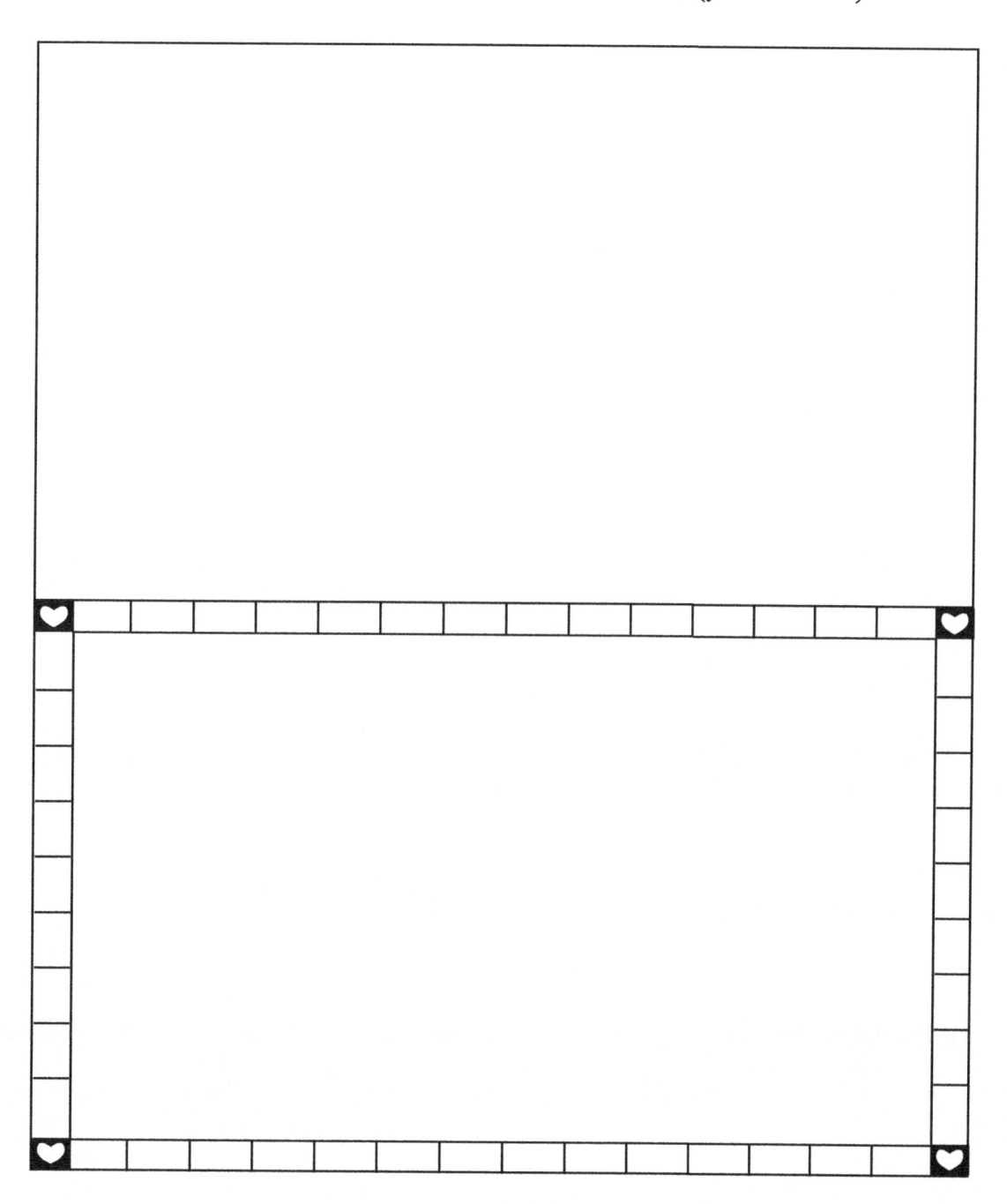

Name

Student Activity Sheet - Week 22

A Pledge is a Promise

I pledge	I promise
allegiance	to be loyal
to the flag	to the symbol that represents our country
of the United States of America,	the joined-together states,
and to the republic for which it stands,	and to the country where the people vote for their leaders,
one nation under God	one country under God
indivisible,	that cannot be separated,
with liberty and justice for all.	that is free and is fair for everyone.

_____
Name

GLOSSARY

WILBUR'S GLOSSARY

A

ACCEPTANCE
Treating everyone I meet with respect, even when they are different from me

APPRECIATION
Recognizing value in people, places and things

APPROPRIATE
Knowing the right thing to say or do

C

CITIZENSHIP
An attitude of cooperation for the good of everyone

CIVIL
Respecting others and myself for the good of our community

CONSCIENTIOUS
Diligently careful

CONSIDERATE
Thinking about the feelings of others before I speak or act

COOPERATION
Choosing to be helpful, not hurtful, when I work with others

COURTESY
Respectful and well-mannered words and actions toward others

E

EMPATHY
Walking in another person's shoes

ENCOURAGEMENT
Offering words to others to build their confidence

EXPRESSIVE
Showing what is in my heart

WILBUR'S GLOSSARY

F

FORGIVENESS
Choosing to let go of bad feelings toward another person

FRIENDLINESS
Welcoming others by offering a quick smile and a kind word

G

GENEROSITY
Gladly giving my time, talent and treasure

GENTLE
Speaking and acting with tenderness

GOODNESS
Being kind and forgiving

GRACIOUS
Being polite, understanding and generous in all situations

GRATEFUL
Giving thanks from the heart

H

HONOR
Showing respect to others because of who they are

HOSPITALITY
Serving others so they feel cared for and comfortable

HUMBLE CONFIDENCE
The courage to be my best so that I can help others become their best

HUMILITY
Not caring who gets credit

K

KINDNESS
Showing care for others in an unexpected and exceptional way

WILBUR'S GLOSSARY

L

LOVE
Genuinely caring for others

LOYALTY
Faithful devotion

M

MANNERS
An attitude of the heart that puts the needs of others ahead of my own

MATURITY
Making the right choice, even when others around me do not

O

OBEDIENCE
Choosing to do what I am told to do

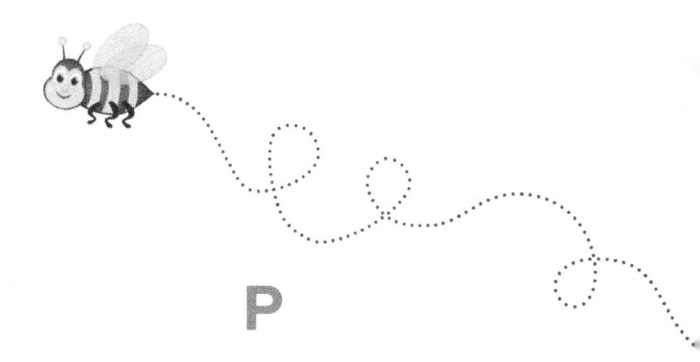

P

PARTICIPATION
Jumping in to do my part

PATIENCE
Choosing to wait without complaining

PATRIOTISM
Loving my country

POLITE
Using kind words and actions

R

RESOURCEFUL
Using my imagination to fix everyday problems

WILBUR'S GLOSSARY

RESPECT
Treating others with dignity

RESPONSIBILITY
Following through on my work without being reminded

S

SELF-CONTROL
Managing myself when no one is looking

SELF-ESTEEM
Self-absorption, presenting itself as self-conceit on one extreme and self-consciousness on the other

SELF-RESPECT
A character trait that results from treating others with dignity

SELFLESS
Giving to others without thinking of myself

SPORTSMANSHIP
Being more concerned with helping my team than helping myself

T

THOUGHTFUL
Looking for ways to make others feel loved

TRUSTWORTHY
Doing what you said you would do when you said you would do it

U

UNDERSTANDING
Accepting others for who they are

The **Education** *of* *the* **HEART**

must be

the **HEART** *of* **Education**

763 North Boulevard, Baton Rouge, LA 70802 — www.mannersoftheheart.org — Phone: 225.383.3235 — Fax: 225.381.3090

Made in the USA
Columbia, SC
05 July 2024